WHERE IS IT?

A TURN-AND-SEE BOOK

by Cari Meister

PEBBLE
a capstone imprint

How do you know where things are? You use position words! Up. Down. In. Out. Left. Right. It's time for you to guess what position word comes next.

Look at each photo. Read the text. Then guess what comes next. Turn the page to find out if you're right!

Carter zooms down the waterslide. Now he is at the **bottom**. Hayden is going next.

Where is Hayden?

turn and see

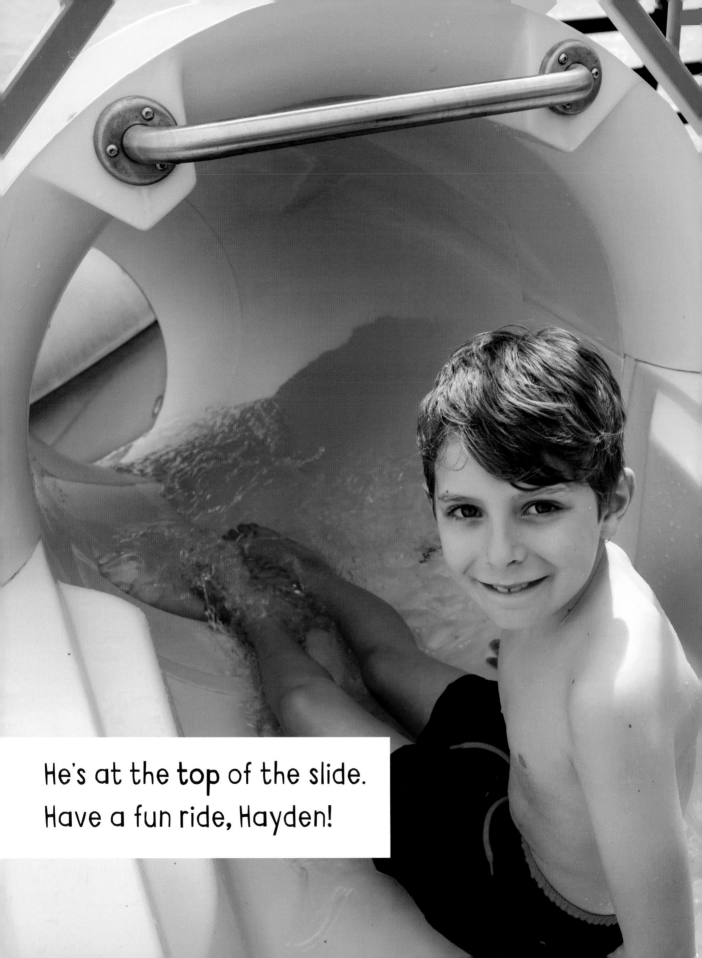

He's at the **top** of the slide.
Have a fun ride, Hayden!

Jax is exploring the aquarium.
Yikes! Here comes a shark!
Thankfully the shark is **inside**
the tank.

Where is Jax?

turn and see

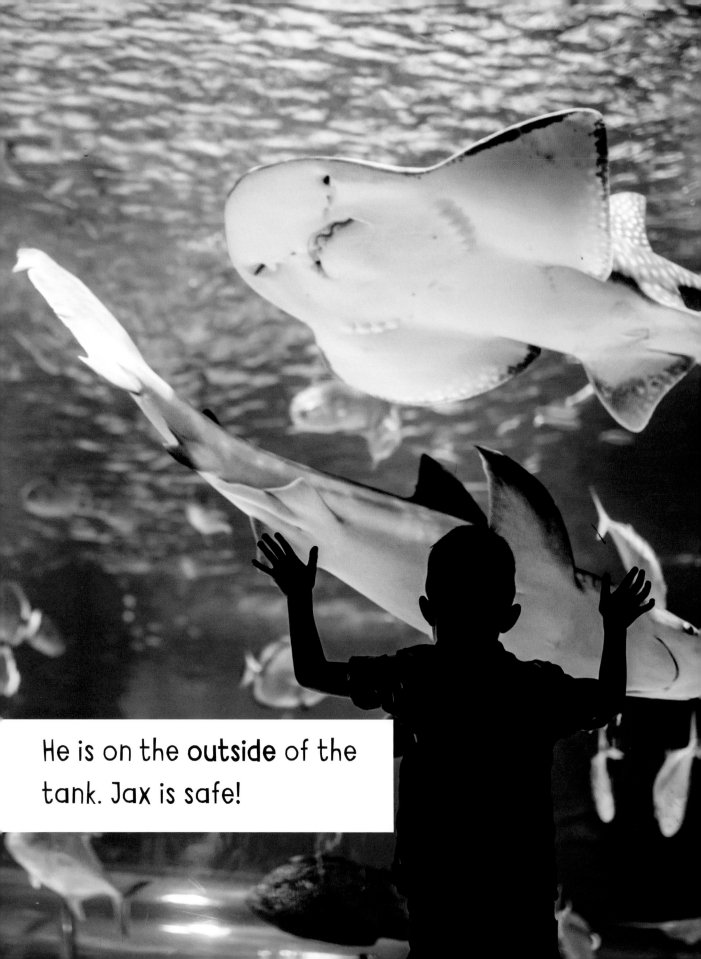

He is on the **outside** of the tank. Jax is safe!

Swoosh! It's a windy spring day.
Gigi is flying her new rainbow
kite. The kite is **above** Gigi.

Where is Gigi?

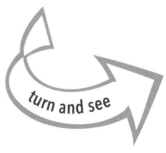

turn and see

She is **below** the kite.
Hold on tight, Gigi!

Joy's class is going to the zoo today! Joy is in the **front** of the line. The rest of the kids line up behind her.

Where is her teacher?

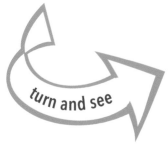

turn and see

She is at the **back** of the line. Maybe she is scared of tigers?

Devon and his friends love to play games. He asks them to hold up a hula hoop. He doesn't jump **over** it. He doesn't crawl **under** it.

Where does Devon go?

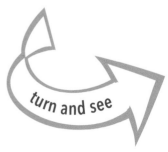

turn and see

Devon goes **through** the hoop!
Great jump, Devon!

The score is tied in the big soccer game. Kiki runs for the ball. She is in **front** of Oscar.

Where is Oscar?

turn and see

He is **behind** Kiki.
Go, Kiki, go!

Hooray! It's the first day of school. Three friends walk to school together. Addie is on the **left**. Gianna is in the **middle**.

Where is Nate?

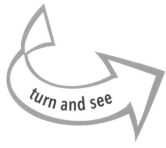
turn and see

Nate is on the **right**. Have fun at school!

Audre and Jalen float over the waves on their tube. Emma and Jack hit a big wave and are no longer on their tube.

Where are Emma and Jack?

turn and see

They are **off** their tube!
Splash!

Wow! Liza and her horse fly **over** the jump without hitting the poles.

Where are the poles?

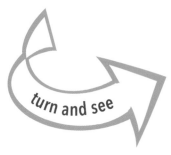

turn and see

The poles are **under** them. Nice jumping, Liza!

It's moving day! Aleema runs into the new house **first**. Her mom comes next.

Where is her dad?

turn and see

He comes in **last**. Aleema can't wait to see her new room!

Theodore and Violet hike **up** the big sledding hill. They jump into their sleds and take off.

Now which way are they going?

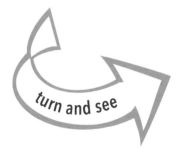

turn and see

Theodore and Violet are zooming **down** the big sledding hill. Whoosh!

It's perfect weather for a camping trip! Ben pitched his tent **near** the peaceful lake. The mountains are across the lake.

Where are the mountains?

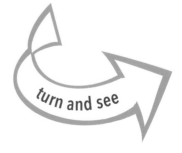
turn and see

The mountains are **far**. Ben better lace up those hiking boots!

On your mark! The runners line up at the **start** of the race. They run and run until they are done.

Where do the runners stop?

turn and see

At the **finish**! Nice job, runners!

Skipper and Buster love to play together. Skipper is **out** of the box. It's way too small for her.

Where is Buster?

turn and see

Buster is in the box!
Aren't they the cutest?

POSITION WORDS REVIEW

- bottom/top
- inside/outside
- above/below
- front/back
- over/under/through
- front/behind
- left/middle/right

- on/off
- over/under
- first/last
- up/down
- near/far
- start/finish
- out/in

Pebble Sprout is published by Pebble, an imprint of Capstone.
1710 Roe Crest Drive
North Mankato, Minnesota 56003
www.capstonepub.com

Library of Congress Cataloging-in-Publication Data
Names: Meister, Cari, author.
Title: Where is it? : a turn-and-see book / by Cari Meister.
Description: North Mankato, Minnesota : Pebble, an imprint of Capstone,
[2021] | Series: Pebble Sprout: What's next? | Audience: Ages 6-8. |
Audience: Grades 2-3. | Summary: "Theodore and Violet trudge up the big
sledding hill. Then they jump in their sleds and take off. Now which way are
they going? You guessed it--down! Keep reading, guessing, and flipping the
page to discover more position words"— Provided by publisher.
Identifiers: LCCN 2020037973 (print) | LCCN 2020037974 (ebook) | ISBN
9781977131577 (hardcover) | ISBN 9781977155344 (ebook pdf) | ISBN
9781977156969 (kindle edition)
Subjects: LCSH: Vocabulary—Juvenile literature. | English language—
Nominals—Juvenile literature. | English language—Grammatical
catagories—Juvenile literature.
Classification: LCC PE1449 .M395 2021 (print) | LCC PE1449 (ebook) | DDC
428.1—dc23
LC record available at https://lccn.loc.gov/2020037973
LC ebook record available at https://lccn.loc.gov/2020037974

Image Credits
Getty Images: FatCamera, 13, 14; kali9, 9, 10; Photo_Concepts, 7, 8;
Shutterstock: Alla Greeg, 27; Denis Moskvinov, 18; fizkes, 21, 22; Grigorta
Ko, cover; LightField Studios, 17; NDAB Creativity, 5, 6; Olga Evans,
28; Phuttharak, 29, 30; Pressmaster, 15, 16; Robert Kneschke, 11, 12;
Romrodphoto, 4; scigelova, 19, 20; simoly, 25, 26; Syda Productions, 23, 24;
VaLiza, 3

Editorial Credits
Editor: Christianne Jones; Designer: Tracy McCabe; Media Researcher:
Morgan Walters; Production Specialist: Kathy McColley

Printed and bound in the USA. 3837